SPORTS
DYNASTIES

D1242507

GENO AURIEMMA

AND THE CONNECTICUT HUSKIES

BY THOMAS CAROTHERS

SportsZone

abdopublishing.com

Published by Abdo Publishing, a division of ABDO, PO Box 398166, Minneapolis, Minnesota 55439.
Copyright © 2019 by Abdo Consulting Group, Inc. International copyrights reserved in all countries.
No part of this book may be reproduced in any form without written permission from the publisher.
SportsZone™ is a trademark and logo of Abdo Publishing.

Printed in the United States of America, North Mankato, Minnesota
042018
092018

THIS BOOK CONTAINS
RECYCLED MATERIALS

Distributed in paperback by North Star Editions, Inc.

Cover Photo: Jessica Hill/AP Images, left; Darron Cummings/AP Images, right
Interior Photos: Elise Amendola/AP Images, 4–5, 15; Robert W Stowell Jr./Archive Photos/Getty Images,
7, 8, 16, 18; Wade Payne/AP Images, 10; John Dunn/AP Images, 12–13; Bob Child/AP Images, 20–21; Mike
Derer/AP Images, 23; Jessica Hill/AP Images, 25, 33, 34, 43; Bill Shettle/Cal Sport Media/AP Images, 26;
Carolyn Kaster/AP Images, 28–29; John Bazemore/AP Images, 31; Stephan Savoia/AP Images, 36–37;
Photo Works/Shutterstock Images, 39; Williams Paul/Icon Sportswire/AP Images, 40

Editor: Bradley Cole
Series Designer: Craig Hinton

Library of Congress Control Number: 2017962591

Publisher's Cataloging-in-Publication Data

Names: Carothers, Thomas, author.
Title: Geno Auriemma and the Connecticut Huskies / by Thomas Carothers.
Description: Minneapolis, Minnesota : Abdo Publishing, 2019. | Series: Sports dynasties | Includes online
    resources and index.
Identifiers: ISBN 9781532114335 (lib.bdg.) | ISBN 9781641852821 (pbk) | ISBN 9781532154164 (ebook)
Subjects: LCSH: Auriemma, Luigi "Geno", 1954-.--Juvenile literature. | Basketball coaches--United States
    --Biography--Juvenile literature. | Women basketball players--United States--Juvenile literature. |
    Connecticut Huskies (Basketball team)--Juvenile literature.
Classification: DDC 796.323092 [B]--dc23

TABLE OF
CONTENTS

CHAPTER 1

BEATING A RIVAL

The University of Connecticut (UConn) women's basketball team had been on the rise for a decade by the 1994–95 season. Head coach Geno Auriemma had guided the Huskies out of the shadows since he arrived in Storrs, Connecticut, in 1985. Every year UConn continued to improve.

The Huskies appeared in their first National Collegiate Athletic Association (NCAA) Tournament in 1989. They advanced to their first

Rebecca Lobo was a key player in helping Connecticut get to the 1995 NCAA championship game.

Final Four in 1991. That was as far as the team had gotten in six tournament trips heading into the 1994–95 season.

But that season, Connecticut soared. The Huskies went undefeated through the regular season and made their second Final Four in 1995. The other three semifinalists had all been to the championship game before. Two of those three, Stanford and Tennessee, had combined to win five national titles.

The Huskies rolled past Stanford 87–60 while Tennessee knocked out Georgia in the semifinals. That left only the Lady Vols between UConn and its first title. Two months earlier, a rivalry had formed between the two teams. Now they were playing for the national championship.

THE START OF A RIVALRY

Tennessee was already one of the country's most dominant women's basketball programs. The Lady Volunteers had participated in every NCAA Tournament since it started in 1982. By 1995 Tennessee had already been to four national finals and won three NCAA championships.

Lobo (50) and her teammates celebrate UConn's first national championship.

But UConn caught up fast. Both teams had participated in every NCAA Tournament since 1989, but they had not played each other until January 16, 1995. No. 1 Tennessee visited the second-ranked Huskies. Tennessee entered that game having won better than 81 percent of its games under head coach Pat Summitt. But the day belonged to UConn, who won 77–66.

Basketball fans around the country waited and hoped that the teams would meet again in the NCAA Tournament. The Final Four that year took place in Minneapolis, Minnesota. The red and blue of Connecticut clashed with the orange and white of Tennessee as the fans filed into Target Center. Everyone wanted to see if the Huskies would finish off an undefeated season or if the Lady Vols would win a fourth national title.

UConn found itself in foul trouble early in the game. Guard Jennifer Rizzotti and forward Rebecca Lobo each picked up two early fouls. With the two All-Americans on the bench, Tennessee took advantage. Guard Laurie Milligan's jump shot gave the Lady Vols a six-point lead going into halftime.

In the second half, the Lady Vols appeared to be pulling away. Tennessee led by nine points. Lobo, UConn's leading scorer, had just six points. But then she began to take over. Lobo scored on four straight possessions to cut Tennessee's lead to one point. Then Rizzotti stole the ball and made a layup to give the Huskies their first lead of the second half.

Pat Summitt, *left*, and Geno Auriemma competed in recruiting just as hard as their teams did on the court.

BRINGING IT HOME

The lead went back and forth after that. With just under four minutes to play, Rizzotti grabbed a rebound, drove the length of the court, and scored on another layup to give the Huskies the lead for good at 63–61. UConn held on to win its first national championship by a final score of 70–64.

The 1995 season kicked off a long rivalry between UConn and Tennessee. The teams battled each other for wins on the court while Auriemma and Summitt battled for recruits off the court.

UConn's defeat of Tennessee placed the Huskies among the great teams in women's basketball. The Lady Vols went on to win an NCAA-record three consecutive national titles from 1996 to 1998. That feat was matched by UConn from 2002 to 2004 and then topped by the Huskies' four-year championship run from 2013 to 2016.

GENO AND PAT

The competition between coaches Geno Auriemma and Pat Summitt fueled the rivalry between UConn and Tennessee. Those schools battled for dominance as the popularity of the game soared. Summitt agreed to play at Connecticut in their first meeting in 1995. However, by 2007 she had decided to end scheduling between the teams.

CHAPTER 2

BUILDING A DYNASTY

For years UConn has been one of the most dominant teams in women's college basketball. But the program came from humble beginnings.

The undefeated 1995 season showed how much the program had grown since it started in 1974. Eight years before the NCAA officially recognized the sport, Connecticut fielded its first women's basketball team. The Huskies finished 2–8 that season, and it didn't get much

The 1995 team finally won Connecticut's first championship.

better for a long time. From 1974 through 1982, UConn had just one winning season while playing in the Yankee Conference. In 1980–81 the Huskies went 16–14.

In 1982–83 women's basketball was finally governed by the NCAA. That year Connecticut left the Yankee Conference for the Big East Conference. But little changed as the Huskies won just nine games in each of the next three seasons, finishing at or near the bottom of the Big East each year.

It was about to get a whole lot better for UConn, however. The Huskies would soon be one of the most successful programs in college basketball history. It all started with the hiring of a dynamic young coach who was destined to become a legend in the sport.

AURIEMMA ARRIVES

The Geno Auriemma era at Connecticut began in May 1985. The *Hartford Courant* announced his hiring with a small mention in the local sports roundup. Auriemma was not well known. His coaching résumé was short. It included four years as an assistant at the University of Virginia and two years as an assistant for the boys' basketball team at his old high school.

The University of Connecticut offered Auriemma his first head coaching position.

The Huskies team he took over was in rough shape. They played in an old gym without locker rooms. They couldn't practice when it rained because the roof leaked so badly. They'd had only one winning season. There was little reason to think that Auriemma and UConn would cause much of a ripple throughout the basketball world.

QUICK TURNAROUND

Auriemma and the Huskies won their first game together on November 23, 1985. Connecticut beat Iona College 73–67. The win was one of a dozen Huskies victories that season as the team again finished with a losing record of 12–15. But it was the last time an Auriemma team would finish below .500 for the season.

Auriemma and assistant coach Chris Dailey gave the Huskies a sense of commitment and hard work starting that first year. In 1987–88 the team went 17–11, 9–7 in the Big East. That was good for fifth place in the conference, and it was a sign of good things to come.

In 1988–89 UConn soared to a 24–6 record and won the Big East with a 13–2 conference mark. That success earned the Huskies their first-ever trip to the NCAA Tournament. Even though eighth-seeded Connecticut lost to ninth-seeded La Salle in the first round, a new level of success had been reached.

Kerry Bascom was Auriemma's first big-name recruit.

SUCCESS GENERATES SUCCESS

The Huskies continued to build their program, and people began to take notice. Auriemma signed his first "blue chip" recruit to a scholarship in 1987. Forward Kerry Bascom was heavily recruited, but she wanted to stay close to her home in New Hampshire, so she chose to play for the Huskies.

The 1998 season saw UConn welcome a "Fab Five" of high school All-Americans to their campus. Tamika Williams, Asjha Jones, Sue Bird, Swin Cash, and Keirsten Walters became known as the "TASSK Force" by Huskies fans. "TASSK" became "TASS" the next season as Walters was unable to play due to knee problems. The remaining "Force" members went on to win national titles in 2000 and 2002. Then Bird (1), Cash (2), Jones (4), and Williams (6) were selected among the top six slots of the 2002 Women's National Basketball Association (WNBA) Draft.

In four years at UConn, Bascom was named the Big East Player of the Year three times, and she earned All-America honors as a senior. Bascom set several team records as the Huskies became a winning program.

Bascom is considered by many as the player who got the ball rolling for Auriemma. In her final season, the Huskies made their first Final Four with a 29–5 record. Bascom started a run of top players signing with the Huskies. Forward Rebecca Lobo, a prep star from Massachusetts, followed Bascom in 1991. Lobo's time in Connecticut ended with the team's first national title in 1995. Since then UConn has consistently landed many of the top high school players in the nation.

CHAPTER 3

STAR PLAYERS

Solid coaching builds the foundation of great programs. The continued success of a great program is fueled by great players. One of Auriemma's first big recruiting wins was signing Rebecca Lobo. The Massachusetts native had been coveted by all of the top programs in the country, but she chose to play at UConn.

The Huskies were knocked out of the NCAA Tournament in the early rounds in Lobo's first two seasons. But they bounced back in her

Coaching and recruiting have built continued success for the Huskies.

junior season. She was named an All-American and led the team to an Elite Eight appearance and its first-ever 30-win season.

Lobo's senior year in 1994–95 was the stuff of dreams. UConn had a perfect 35–0 season and won its first national title. By this point Lobo was one of the most recognizable faces in the sport. She led the Huskies to the title. During her senior year, she scored 17.1 points and grabbed 9.8 rebounds per game to cap an amazing four-year career. She was named the Associated Press Female Athlete of the Year and the NCAA Women's Basketball Player of the Year.

While Lobo was raised in New England, the Huskies' next superstar came to Connecticut from the opposite side of the country. Diana Taurasi differed greatly from Lobo in where she grew up, but both helped make UConn a national power.

In the fall of 2000, Diana Taurasi traveled across the country from California to play guard for Connecticut. The Huskies were coming off their second national title. While Taurasi's freshman season ended with a loss in the Final Four, she bounced back to lead UConn to national titles the next three years. Auriemma directly credited Taurasi with the Huskies' success. When asked

Diana Taurasi was the leader of three straight UConn championship teams.

in 2004 about UConn's dominance, the coach simply said, "We have Diana, and you don't."

Taurasi had a cocky attitude that made her popular with her teammates and hated by her rivals. She became known as one of the most clutch players to put on a UConn jersey. Taurasi's success was the product of a mix of raw talent and an insatiable desire to win. She became the team's first two-time Naismith College Player of the Year honoree, winning the awards in 2003 and 2004. Her record with the Huskies was 139–8, and

Nykesha Sales was one of the Huskies' star players in the late 1990s. She was a two-time All-American in 1996–97 and 1997–98. She was a member of UConn's first national championship team in 1995, and the Huskies won at least 30 games in each of her four seasons in Storrs. The Big East Conference Player of the Year in her senior season of 1997–98, Sales graduated as UConn's all-time leading scorer at the time with 2,178 points.

Connecticut posted its second undefeated season in 2002–03, going 39–0 during Taurasi's sophomore year.

Taurasi was known for being able to back up big talk with big plays. She took that trait to the WNBA after the Phoenix Mercury chose her No. 1 overall in the 2004 WNBA draft.

REGAINING MOMENTUM

The program hit a lull by UConn's standards after Taurasi left. The Huskies failed to reach the Final Four three straight years. Then Maya Moore arrived in 2007 and changed everything.

A star guard from Lawrenceville, Georgia, Moore came to UConn with a winning reputation after going 125–3 as a four-year starter at Collins Hill High School. After winning three state titles, Moore brought her winning ways to UConn and helped propel the team back to the top. She and the Huskies cut down the nets again after back-to-back 39–0 seasons in

Maya Moore set many records during her time at UConn.

2008–09 and 2009–10. UConn set a new college basketball winning streak of 90 games that stretched into Moore's senior season in 2010–11. Overall, Moore's teams went a combined 150–4 in her four years at Connecticut.

Breanna Stewart was one of the best ever to play for the Huskies.

Moore earned multiple national player of the year honors during her collegiate career. She left UConn as its all-time leading scorer, and No. 4 in NCAA history, with 3,036 points. She was chosen by the Minnesota Lynx as the first pick of the

2011 WNBA Draft. Moore had arguably the greatest career of any Huskies player to that point. Many wondered who the next superstar would be. They did not have to wait long to find an answer.

Breanna Stewart was a power forward out of Syracuse, New York. She became the most dominant player of UConn's most dominant era. Like Moore, Stewart was a national player of the year honoree. However, she bettered Moore's record by winning four national championships. Stewart, named the Final Four Most Outstanding Player four times, went 151–5 at UConn. During her junior season, the Huskies began a record-shattering 111-game winning streak.

Stewart was a powerful force in the Huskies frontcourt. But she also ran the floor and involved her teammates like a guard. She was one of only six Huskies to finish her college career with more than 1,000 points and 1,000 assists. She finished with 2,676 points, second only to Moore in team history. After becoming the first woman to be named the consensus national player of the year three times, Stewart was the No. 1 pick of the 2016 WNBA Draft, selected by the Seattle Storm.

CHAPTER 4

BREAKING
RECORDS

U Conn has a habit of winning championships in bunches. The Huskies won three straight NCAA titles from 2002 to 2004. Then they won back-to-back championships in 2009 and 2010. But their most successful stretch came from 2013 through 2016, when they won four national titles in four years.

That run got off to a slow start in 2012–13. UConn suffered four defeats that season, including three losses to rival Notre Dame.

The Huskies met President Barack Obama in 2016 after winning their fourth straight NCAA title.

However, the Huskies had the final word against the Irish with an 83–65 win in the national semifinal. After dispatching their top rival, the Huskies walloped Louisville 93–60 in the title game to embark on the four-title run. The win improved UConn to 8–0 in NCAA championship games.

The Huskies capped a 40–0 season with the 2014 championship. UConn bested Maryland in the semifinals before beating Notre Dame 79–58 for the championship. The Huskies were dominant the entire season. The closest they came to losing all year was an 11-point win over Baylor in early January. The Huskies held the No. 1 ranking in the country from start to finish that season.

In November 2014, Connecticut suffered its first loss in 21 months when it fell 88–86 in overtime at Stanford. However, the setback was a small bump in the road as the Huskies rolled to their third straight championship with a 38–1 record. UConn downed a familiar opponent for that season's title, defeating Notre Dame 63–53 in the championship game.

Another 38–0 undefeated season wrapped up the run. For the fourth straight title, UConn beat Oregon State in the national semifinals before defeating Syracuse 82–51 in the

Though their winning streak was snapped, the Huskies still got to celebrate the 2014 championship.

title game. The Orange were playing in their first NCAA final, whereas the Huskies remained perfect at 11–0 in national championship games.

THE 90-GAME WINNING STREAK

UConn is known for its record-setting winning streaks. UConn holds the three longest winning streaks in women's college basketball history. First the Huskies set an NCAA record with a 90-game winning streak. It began with an 82–71 home win over Georgia Tech in the 2008–09 season opener. UConn was coming off a loss to Stanford in the previous season's Final Four. The Huskies would not lose again until Stanford defeated them 71–59 on December 31, 2010.

Ten days before the loss to Stanford, UConn made NCAA history with its 89th straight win. That victory broke the NCAA record for longest winning streak, set by the men's team at the University of California, Los Angeles (UCLA). The Bruins won 88 straight games from 1971 to 1974.

Breaking UCLA's streak was such a big deal that Auriemma received a call from President Barack Obama. Greg Wooden was on hand to congratulate Auriemma after the record-breaking win. He is the grandson of John Wooden, the legendary head coach of those great UCLA Bruins teams.

THE 111-GAME WINNING STREAK

The Huskies smashed that mark by not losing a game for almost three full seasons before Mississippi State upset them in the 2017 title game. Amazingly, UConn nearly put together a 158-game winning streak. The Huskies won 46 straight before losing to Stanford in overtime in the second game of the 2014–15 season. Then they won their next 111 games.

Greg Wooden, grandson of John Wooden, was in attendance when UConn broke UCLA's record for longest winning streak.

The first of the 111 straight victories was a 96–90 win over visiting Creighton on November 23, 2014. From that point, UConn won every game the rest of that season, went undefeated the next season, and remained perfect throughout

the 2016–17 schedule until the loss to Mississippi State. The Huskies were so dominant in this stretch that only three games out of the 111 wins were decided by fewer than 10 points.

All three of those games came in the final season of the streak, after the graduation of star players Breanna Stewart, Morgan Tuck, and Moriah Jefferson, who formed the backbone of the four-time championship squads.

Along the way came three American Athletic Conference (AAC) titles and two national championships. The streak lasted 867 days and remains the longest winning run in the history of NCAA sports.

GAMPEL PAVILION

Before 1990 Connecticut played in an old field house that seated fewer than 5,000 people. That all changed with the opening of the Gampel Pavilion. The arena seats nearly 10,000 fans for both the Huskies men's and women's basketball teams. The arena was the setting for UConn's 77–66 defeat of No. 1-ranked Tennessee on January 16, 1995.

CHAPTER 5

CONTINUED SUCCESS

Connecticut's lasting dynasty has helped launch the careers of many players and coaches. Several UConn players have gone on to professional success both on and off the court.

Rebecca Lobo continued to be a major influence in women's basketball both on and off the court. After she graduated from UConn, Lobo won a gold medal with Team USA

Rebecca Lobo was inducted into the Naismith Basketball Hall of Fame in 2017.

at the 1996 Atlanta Olympics. The next year she joined the New York Liberty for the inaugural WNBA season.

Lobo helped lead the Liberty to the WNBA Finals in 1998, but her professional career was hampered by knee injuries. Lobo left the court for the broadcast booth after her professional basketball career came to an end in 2003. She serves as an announcer and analyst for WNBA television broadcasts.

Lobo was inducted into the Women's Basketball Hall of Fame in 2010. In 2017 she was enshrined in the Naismith Memorial Basketball Hall of Fame for her contributions to the game as a player and broadcaster.

BIRD TAKES FLIGHT

Sue Bird graduated from Connecticut in 2002 and went on to become one of the biggest superstars of the WNBA. Bird became the first Huskies player to be taken first overall in the WNBA draft when the Seattle Storm selected her in 2002.

Bird helped guide the team to the WNBA title in 2004. That made her one of just six players ever to win an NCAA championship, a WNBA title, and an Olympic gold medal.

Tina Charles played for both the University of Connecticut and the Connecticut Suns.

She had been part of the victorious USA Basketball team at the 2004 Athens Olympics. Bird went on to win another WNBA title in 2010 and three more gold medals in 2008, 2012, and 2016, the last two with Auriemma as the US head coach. She is also the league's all-time assist leader.

The second pick of the 2002 WNBA Draft, chosen right after Bird, was UConn's Swin Cash. The hard-working forward won three league titles with the Detroit Shock and Seattle Storm.

Cash played in four WNBA All-Star games and won two All-Star Most Valuable Player (MVP) trophies. She also joined Bird in the NCAA-WNBA-Olympic gold medal club. Cash played on gold-medal-winning USA teams in the 2004 Athens Olympics and the 2012 London Olympics.

Cash retired in 2016 after becoming the second player in WNBA history to record at least 5,000 points, 2,000 rebounds, and 1,000 assists in her career. In 2017 the New York Liberty named Cash the team's Director of Franchise Development. She became just the second WNBA player to assume a front-office position after retirement.

HOMETOWN HERO

Tina Charles graduated from UConn in 2010 as the leading scorer and rebounder in program history. Then she was selected first overall by the Connecticut Sun in the WNBA Draft. Charles won the 2010 WNBA Rookie of the Year Award. She went on to be named the league's MVP in 2012. Charles won Olympic gold medals with Team USA in 2012 and 2016.

After winning two WNBA titles with the Houston Comets, Jennifer Rizzotti began her coaching career at the University of Hartford. She earned three conference coach of the year honors there before taking over the George Washington University program in 2016. Rizzotti has also coached at the U18 and U19 level for USA Basketball. She was named USA Basketball National Coach of the Year in 2011.

CHRIS DAILEY

Chris Dailey came to Connecticut as Auriemma's assistant coach in 1985. She had previously served as an assistant at Rutgers. Dailey has stayed with Auriemma and UConn despite receiving several head coaching offers over the years. Dailey refers to herself as a "teacher." One of her specialties is providing support to players on the bench during games.

Auriemma named Dailey associate head coach in 1998, and he's said he views her as an equal partner in the program's success. She has taken her turn as the team's head coach on multiple occasions. UConn won Big East Conference Tournament titles under her direction in 1989 and 1997 when Auriemma was absent.

The Auriemma-Daley combo has taken UConn to unprecedented heights. They won't remain in Storrs forever,

Chris Dailey has passed up head coaching opportunities to stay at Connecticut.

and whoever replaces them probably won't win 11 national titles. But they've set up Huskies basketball to remain a powerhouse for years to come.

UNIVERSITY OF CONNECTICUT HUSKIES

SPAN OF DYNASTY

- 1994–95 to present

NATIONAL CHAMPIONSHIPS

- 11 (1995, 2000, 2002, 2003, 2004, 2009, 2010, 2013, 2014, 2015, 2016)

KEY RIVALS

- Tennessee, Stanford, Notre Dame

GENO AURIEMMA RECORDS

- Overall (through 2017–18): 991–135
- Big East: 472–61
- AAC: 101–0

NCAA TOURNAMENT

- NCAA Tournament Appearances: 31
- NCAA Tournament Titles: 11
- Conference Championships: Big East 19, AAC 6

AURIEMMA AWARDS

- Big East Coach of the Year, 10
- AAC Coach of the Year, 4
- National Coach of the Year, 8
- USA Women's Basketball Coach of the Year, 6

INDIVIDUAL HONORS

ASSOCIATED PRESS NATIONAL PLAYER OF THE YEAR

- Rebecca Lobo (1995)
- Jennifer Rizzotti (1996)
- Kara Wolters (1997)
- Sue Bird (2002)
- Diana Taurasi (2003)
- Maya Moore (2009, 2011)
- Tina Charles (2010)
- Breanna Stewart (2014, 2015, 2016)

WNBA FIRST OVERALL DRAFT PICKS

- Sue Bird
  Seattle Storm (2002)
- Diana Taurasi
  Phoenix Mercury (2003)
- Tina Charles
  Connecticut Sun (2010)
- Maya Moore
  Minnesota Lynx (2011)
- Breanna Stewart
  Seattle Storm (2016)

MAY 17, 1985

UConn hires Geno Auriemma as head coach.

MARCH 15, 1989

UConn plays its first NCAA Tournament game, a 72–63 loss to La Salle.

MARCH 30, 1991

The Huskies reach their first NCAA Final Four.

JANUARY 16, 1995

The Huskies win their first meeting with Tennessee, 77–66 at Gampel Pavilion.

APRIL 2, 1995

The Huskies win their first national title with a 70–64 defeat of Tennessee.

APRIL 6, 2004

The Huskies win their third consecutive national championship.

DECEMBER 21, 2010

UConn tops the UCLA men's record winning streak with its 89th straight win.

APRIL 5, 2016

The Huskies win their fourth consecutive national championship.

MARCH 27, 2017

UConn wins its national-record 111th consecutive game.

MARCH 30, 2018

UConn's 19th Final Four appearance ends with a 91–89 overtime loss to Notre Dame in the national semifinals.

ALL-AMERICAN

An athlete honored as one of the best amateurs in the United States.

BLUE CHIP

A player of the highest quality.

CONSECUTIVE

In unbroken sequence.

CONSENSUS

A general agreement.

FINAL FOUR

The semifinal round of the NCAA basketball tournament.

FRESHMAN

A first-year player.

INFLUENCE

Having an effect on the development or behavior of someone or something.

INSATIABLE

Impossible to satisfy.

RECRUIT

A high school player who is being convinced to attend a certain college, usually to play a sport.

RIVAL

An opponent with whom a player or team has a fierce and ongoing competition.

SANCTIONED

Given permission or approval for an action.

ONLINE RESOURCES

Booklinks
NONFICTION NETWORK
FREE! ONLINE NONFICTION RESOURCES

To learn more about Geno Auriemma and the Connecticut Huskies, visit abdobooklinks.com. These links are routinely monitored and updated to provide the most current information available.

BOOKS

Axon, Rachel. *Title IX Levels the Playing Field*. Minneapolis, MN: Abdo Publishing, 2018.

Ervin, Phil. *Maya Moore: WNBA Champion*. Minneapolis, MN: Abdo Publishing, 2016.

Kortemeier, Todd. *The Greatest Female Athletes of All Time*. Minneapolis, MN: Abdo Publishing, 2018.

INDEX

ABOUT THE AUTHOR

Thomas Carothers has been a sportswriter for the past 15 years in the Minneapolis/ St. Paul, Minnesota, area. He has worked for a number of print and online publications, mostly focusing on prep sports coverage. He lives in Minneapolis with his wife and a house full of dogs.